✛ AN OBSERVER'S GUIDE

Pencil Drawing

Pencil Drawing

John C. Brobbel, A.R.B.A.

FREDERICK WARNE

Published by Frederick Warne (Publishers) Ltd, London, 1981

© Frederick Warne (Publishers) Ltd 1981

To dearest Carol
'Hope, love, joy are poesy.'
(Clare)

Acknowledgements

The British Museum: Constable and Ingres drawings; Carol E. Gardner;
Pauline Sandor.

ISBN 0 7232 2470 6

Filmset and Printed in Great Britain
by BAS Printers Limited, Over Wallop, Hampshire
1502.1180

Contents

Introduction

Though concentrating on pencil as its medium, much of the advice and instruction contained within these pages is common to any form of drawing from observation.

Primarily learning to draw is learning to see anew those everyday things usually taken for granted. Much of the environment is so familiar that when it comes before the eyes it is so 'usual' that it ceases to be regarded as anything other than ordinary. This cursory attitude to what we are surrounded by, and part of, makes learning to draw that much more difficult.

Though much seen is familiar it does not follow that it is known. Unless we have a particular interest in something there will be much that goes unseen. Learning to be a good draughtsman involves, above everything else, a sensitivity and awareness of the visual order of all you happen upon. Except in very few instances this state of awareness and sensitivity is the result of a great deal of hard and lengthy study.

It will not be an easy task, and unfortunately there are no short cuts for the impatient. It is, however, an activity which is never boring or tedious, and a striving nature, so much a part of creativity, can after a while inspire both exploration and discovery of a vision of the world that is both unique and personal.

Though the instruction contained within these pages may be useful, and the advice worth trusting in (on occasions!), any teaching is limited; apart from reading this type of manual you may find much benefit in attending an evening class in drawing, and perusing as many original works as possible

How sensitive you become towards your chosen subject is the key to any poetic content your work will have; in time this vital element will be discovered. However, if you are going to achieve any success with your drawing you must be prepared to work very hard at it and try to be patient. Henry Tonks, who taught drawing at the Slade School at the beginning of the century to many subsequently notable artists (including Augustus John, Stanley Spencer and Tom Monnington), was a teacher of great enthusiasm and integrity. His idea was that:

What makes painting the best of all possible sports is that we have to fix our minds so entirely on the difficulties of doing, that we have no time to look after the essential thing, the poetry that looks after itself, or does not, as the case may be.

This still holds true today.

For many people, learning to draw will, by necessity, be a spare-time activity. However, this should not mean that your attitude towards your work is a spare-time one, engaged in lightly to pass the time. Even when not in the turmoil of creating, it is vital to be continuously aware of drawing. Keep on the alert for suitable subjects, and incidentally, unsuitable ones. This important aspect will be discussed at a later stage.

Though drawing, in the sense that these pages discuss, is our response to the visual world, and therefore an emotional one, it will be more helpful to your development if you set about your work with some sort of order and logic. An unhurried and careful approach, which is not too ambitious, will reap the most benefit. Always remember that as you will be learning mistakes will be frequent. Try to be patient, because once control is lost in your drawing it will be difficult to re-establish.

Drawing reveals the measure of our visual understanding, and sympathy with the subject. Approaching drawing with a genuine desire to understand the different visual structures of subjects will in time teach the significance of these elements in the creating of painting and sculpture. How does the pattern on a lace tablecloth distort and change when it is hanging from a nail on a wall? What happens to the smooth glass-like surface of a lake when the wind blows, or a motorboat and skier pass through it? Searching for the answers to these sort of questions, and others, will help you to understand that although things change, they always have a visual structure and an underlying logic. The draughtsman has to discover and re-create these elusive aspects.

Drawing is something which, especially at the beginning, may be very exhausting; and when one is not achieving the desired result, it can be disheartening. There will be many disappointing drawing sessions ahead, but perseverance and effort will bring better days. I stress this because it is important that you begin with the right attitude towards your work. During a now-famous court action between the American artist J. M. McNeil Whistler and the art critic John Ruskin, Whistler, having stated two days as the length of time it took him to paint 'Nocturne in Black and Gold' was then asked by Counsel '. . . and that was the labour for which you asked two hundred guineas?' to which he replied 'No, it was for the knowledge gained through a lifetime.'

The work which you will be producing, no matter how many people recognise it, if it is serious and honest work, will be a contribution to twentieth-century drawing.

A desire to create is inherent in us all. The teaching of art in schools is limited, and in some cases seems no more than an extra period of recreation. Why art should suffer in this way remains a mystery to many artists who believe that consciousness through art is vital to any progress in education and, indeed, civilisation.

Materials

The versatility and convenience of the lead pencil makes it ideal for the beginner to drawing. It can be used both for broad tonal work and also very fine line work. Its range of tone is comprehensive and drawings made with a number of different grades can be very satisfying, covering the full tonal scale. It is small, compact and can be carried unobtrusively at almost any time. Though I deal, in the main, with lead pencils in these pages, there are of course other types such as carbon, charcoal and coloured pencils. However, if the lead pencil can be mastered, it is only a matter of making slight adjustments to familiarise oneself with the characteristics of the others.

The term 'lead pencil' is not strictly correct as a description of this implement. The pencils are, in fact, made from a mixture of graphite and clay. The process was invented in 1709 by a Frenchman called Conté, so it is a fairly modern tool. Real lead pencils were used in the fifteenth century for preliminary work on unprepared paper for pen and ink and chalk drawings, as they left only a faint image. The pencil drawings most familiar to us date from the time of Conté's discovery. The pencil has to some extent replaced the use of pen and ink, crayon and silver point (a method of drawing using a sharpened stick of silver on prepared paper, which gives a very delicate and even line) as the most popular medium for draughting in the fine arts.

Pencils

The materials which will be required are few, and relatively easy to obtain. To begin with a variety of different grades of pencil will be needed. Though the range is quite expansive, for our purposes we need only concern ourselves with the middle ones. These are HB, B, 2B and 3B. The HB is useful for light construction lines and fine detailed work. The B grade is most helpful for making quick notes, perhaps when time is limited, and is particularly useful as it is hard enough to be used in a fine linear way, yet still soft enough to give an adequate and even range of tone. The most commonly used grade is the 2B, which is excellent for tonal drawings, but 2B pencils do tend to lose their points rather quickly. A 3B is an excellent grade for producing very dark areas, and accents. When used on its own it is best employed in a broad manner, as any point will soon lose its sharpness with the lead being so soft.

Paper

The next important consideration should be paper. As a general rule lead pencil produces its best qualities on a fairly smooth hot pressed cartridge paper. A heavy-grained paper, though useful for certain subjects, should be avoided at first, as the grain tends to come through any tonal areas and creates a mechanical texture, often where one is not required. Should you wish to experiment with grained papers, however, you will find that generally the heavier the grain and more expensive the paper, the harder the grade of pencil should be. For instance, a B grade pencil on high quality paper often produces a much softer line and becomes smudgier; in fact its qualities become akin to those of a 2B pencil used on a smoother cartridge paper. Good quality pencils and paper are well worth the few extra pence, so always try to use the best.

Erasers

Though erasers are frowned upon by many teachers and artists, used correctly they can be of some significance. They can help to knock down a line or area of tone which has become too dark, and so reads too importantly in your drawing. Also when drawing with the softer grades of pencil you will find, especially while inexperienced, that smudges will appear over parts of the paper which you wish to leave as highlights in the drawing; an eraser can be used to pick out these areas. Never attempt to obliterate areas of drawing by rubbing out. Mistakes are very important to the future development of the student and this reason, apart from any other, should be sufficient to keep you from using an eraser indiscriminately. So, if you must use one at all, use a good quality kneadable rubber, keep it clean, and above all, use it intelligently.

Drawing boards

Drawing boards are all manufactured in standard sizes so no difficulty should be found in choosing a suitably-sized one. An imperial size board and half imperial are the most suitable. It is worth shopping around for a good quality board of soft wood. The best are those made up with narrow strips joined together by two cross-pieces on the back. A single sheet is liable to distort and warp.

If your budget will not stretch to such a luxury and you decide to make a cheaper board, do not use hardboard, as this will not take the thumb tacks used for securing the paper. A fairly acceptable substitute for a manufactured drawing board (and extra light) is fibre board. This is relatively cheap and is best for a half imperial size or smaller board; it can be cut with a sharp knife. Remember to make your dimensions a minimum 25 mm (1 in) larger each way than the paper size intended for it. I use this kind of board for outdoor work and find it most satisfactory. Keep it dry, as it will not survive too much moisture.

Miscellaneous items

Other items required include a pencil holder, in which can be inserted those pencils which have been whittled below half length. This small addition is well worth the investment. A pencil smaller than about 10 cm (4 in) can be a very awkward instrument.

A sharp knife with a retractable blade is probably the best for sharpening your pencils. The Stanley-knife type is ideal and useful too, for mounting your work at a later stage. I find this type the most reliable for keeping its edge the longest.

Best quality thumb tacks are essential; next best are metal clips to keep the paper immovable on the drawing board. Cheap thumb tacks have a tendency to break off at the head, and apart from being painful to the thumb, you will find the remaining headless pin is difficult to remove without resorting to a pair of pliers.

Sketchbooks

Carrying a sketchbook whenever possible, and using it even for the quickest notations, will be a source of endless pleasure, as well as a most useful store of information. Its value is immense, and lies in using it not as a bound portfolio for exhibition, but in the collecting of ideas and notation of small important details which may come in useful for future paintings. A sketchbook can be used to collect information such as reflections in windows, chimney stacks, lamp posts, any subjects which can be assessed in a fairly short time, for example while waiting for public transport. They are immensely useful for notation of poses people and groups of figures naturally take up.

A useful hint for use with sketchbooks is to have an elastic band around each cover which you may pull over the edge of a page, so keeping it flat in windy weather.

A straight stick about 30 cm (12 in) long, such as a piece of thin dowel rod, will be used for measurement and the finding of angles. This will be discussed in detail at a later stage. You will also need a sheet of fine sandpaper for pencil sharpening.

A page from a sketchbook

Fixative

This is used to literally 'fix' the pencil marks to the paper. It can be bought in aerosol form or a little more cheaply in a bottle. A diffuser must be used with the bottle. When a drawing is completed hold it vertical and spray it with fixative from a distance of about 20–30 cm (9–12 in) evenly all over. This stops the drawing from smudging. Never use fixative in a confined space.

When these items have been acquired you have all you need to begin. There are many ways that you can use a pencil and all of them have their own particular role in drawing. Some of these depend on how you sharpen your pencil. A well-kept point is essential if you are going to produce drawings of any quality and character. There are two types of point which you may find useful. The first and most common is a simple tapering of the pencil to a very fine point. The other is a similar tapering of the pencil, but instead of a very fine point, the lead is sanded down to a chisel shape.

Always use a sharp edge when pencil sharpening. Begin by whittling away the surrounding wood about 25 mm (1 in) from its end, tapering evenly. If this operation is carried out correctly there should be about two-thirds bare wood, the other third exposed lead. You can either continue to sharpen the lead to its desired point with the knife or use the sandpaper. The chisel shape is cut in the same fashion, but instead of rubbing the lead part at an angle and rotating it to achieve the even tapering, the pencil should be held at an angle rigid between 30–40 degrees and rubbed on the sandpaper until a flat plane is achieved. The chisel shape gives a thicker yet still very even line, and of course can be useful for textures.

13

Remember not to chop at the wood; carve it away slowly. Once sharpening the pencil correctly has been mastered it will become much faster. If insufficient lead is exposed or a permanently blunt point is maintained it will be difficult to achieve the complete range of marks and qualities of the medium. All this fuss about sharpening may appear to some as superfluous, but if you are going to proceed with any degree of professionalism, then you must be able to prepare and use your tools correctly and know and respect them.

To continue with learning about your materials I would suggest that readers who have not seriously attempted drawing since their schooldays familiarise themselves with their pencils before attempting anything too ambitious.

Many students at first hold a pencil in the same way that they would when writing characters. This is not always suitable when making drawings, except when working on small areas and details. Essentially, when writing characters the tendency is to use wrist action. For drawing, the marks which are used are longer and more varied. What must be learnt is the use of the arm as an extension of the pencil, in effect drawing with the whole action of the arm, the shoulder being the pivot. This action, though a little strange to begin with, is soon learnt and gives greater control over the pencil, as well as freeing one from the tense way one holds a writing implement. Do not press on to the paper; there is no need as the lead will leave an image with very little pressure. Keep your elbow away from your body and do not grip the pencil too tightly. Study the position of your fingers when holding the pencil for different lines. Practising simple strokes and experimenting with different textures will help you to get the feel of the pencil and the differing qualities of the grades and points.

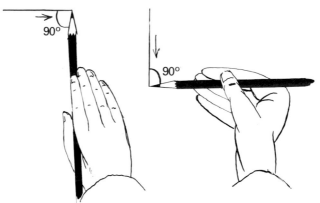

Getting the feel of the pencil; the arm is an extension of the pencil

The following exercise should suffice to break the ice. Draw a grid as follows: using the HB pencil draw a series of horizontal parallel lines. Start about 25 mm (1 in) from either the top edge or the bottom edge of the paper. What concerns us here is not the actual line, but that the space between it and the edge of the paper remains constant and each subsequent space too. Make the spaces approximately 25 mm (1 in) apart. Repeat this with vertical lines until the paper is divided up into roughly equal squares. It does not matter if the lines are a little uneven, providing their general direction is kept. If you find that you are quite hopeless and your line is wandering, check first that you are holding the pencil correctly. It may be helpful to stage-draw your lines if you still cannot get them right. All this means is that you plot the distance between long lines by drawing a series of shorter ones, each joining onto the previous one.

This way of constructing one line from a number of points will not help you to draw straight lines particularly, but it will help you to be aware of distances and how to establish them in an unobtrusive way. It is sometimes referred to as 'point to point' drawing, and its usefulness lies in the fact that it will help you to gauge relationships much more accurately.

It is with relationships of one shape against another, lines against one another and tonal values (that is shading) that the difficulties of drawing occur time after time. It is comparatively easy to draw straight lines, so if we can learn how to achieve this in a fairly short time then why is it such a

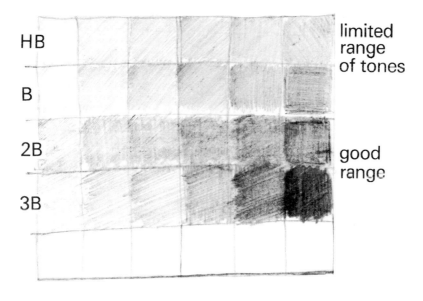

HB

B

2B

3B

limited
range
of tones

good
range

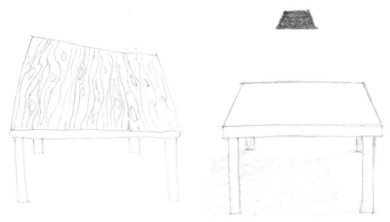

The difficulties of drawing in isolation

problem to draw objects? The answer is that any mark which is made must relate to what it is next to on the paper.

Many students draw in isolation. At the outset in single studies it is single lines which do not relate to one another – for example, the edges of a table top. The novice relates the line actually in the process of being drawn only to the line being copied and not to the previous line or general big shape. This is why it is always worthwhile stopping every so often and comparing the shapes on your paper with those of the subject. For most beginners this only happens when the drawing has been completed, and then the mistakes are usually so numerous that a new drawing must be begun.

Once this problem is solved and more than one object constitutes the subject, the novice falls into exactly the same trap, except instead of drawing edges in the wrong place he tends to draw each part of the subject in isolation; the effect is that each individual object is well drawn but not related to its neighbours. Much of this problem can be resolved by a recognition of shapes which you cannot pick up – the negative shapes which are created by the boundaries of positive ones. So, rather than viewing the distance between objects as empty space look for the shape which fills the space and draw that. The identification of negative shape comes in very useful when drawing foreshortened figures.

Measurement

The piece of dowel listed earlier is used for comparing sizes and checking whether your angles are correct. The way to use this very simple aid is as follows: hold it as in the diagram using your thumb as a sliding measure. Now hold it out in front of you at arm's length between you and whatever

16

you wish to measure. Close one eye, and line up the top of the stick with one extremity of the distance being measured; then keeping your arm steady and the stick vertical slide your thumb along until it is in line with the opposite end of the distance you wish to measure. You now have a comparative measurement, which is known as sight size.

If you measure the two sides of a square straight on, the horizontal and vertical measurements taken this way should correspond to each other. Indeed it is best to use this method of measuring only to check proportions, rather than attempting to transfer the actual measurements from the measuring stick to paper. Do remember though to hold the stick in the same hand each time you measure, and do not bend your arm. If you take two measurements of the same distance, one with a straight arm and one with it bent, then you will see why this is important.

The closer the object the larger the measurement. So a matchbox in the foreground of your picture may actually be represented by a shape occupying more area of your drawing than a large book set back in the composition.

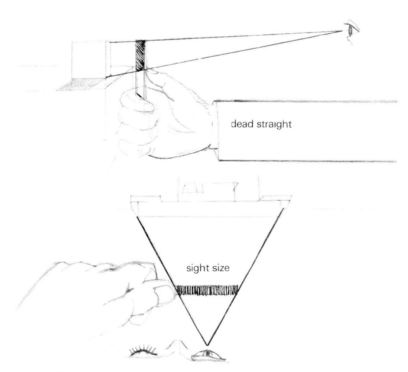

Using the dowel to take comparative measurement or sight size

Reasons and attitudes

There are many advantages that come with an ability to draw. Not only a sense of purpose and insight into nature, but others too. It will help you to be better equipped to understand and appreciate a wider scope of creativity, and the work of other artists. The concentrated nature of drawing makes it an activity almost entirely geared to thought, and as such it is to many artists a whole philosophy. During a lecture John Constable, one of the most well-known of English landscape artists, spoke of painting as being scientific as well as poetic:

> Why, then, may not landscape drawing be considered as a branch of natural philosophy, of which pictures are but experiments?

The attitude underlying this statement is not without humility in that the artist has learnt sufficient about nature to be genuinely awed by its magnitude and significance and knows that by its study he can learn much.

In the same lecture Constable said:

> . . . what are the most sublime productions of the pencil but selections of some of the forms of nature, and copies of a few of her effervescent effects; and this is the result, not of inspiration, but of long and patient study, under the direction of much good sense . . .

Discovery of the visual world around us and study of its myriad moods and influences must play an important role in any artist's philosophy, and without this being an integral part of your studies the work you produce will never progress past a superficial facility.

The many beautiful portraits which the seventeenth-century artist Rembrandt van Rijn painted are among the most searching and revealing portraits which have ever been made. Rembrandt was an artist who studied his subjects very intensely and often worked for great lengths of time on his paintings. Only by careful and thoughtful study, and an intense regard for his sitters was he able to produce such soulful and imaginative work.

Drawing affects all our lives, and is perhaps one of the most fundamental activities with which we all have to occupy ourselves at some time. Almost

John Constable. *Pencil study of trees* (British Museum)

everything created by man has been conceived and first expressed in two-dimensional terms, from the tools which help dig our vegetables from the earth, to the table from which we eat.

The reasons for drawing vary considerably and it is worth noting why we want to make two-dimensional grey and black representations of three-dimensional objects. It may be to help our memory to recall a place once visited, or a particular object we may not have the chance to see again. Perhaps the reason for picking up a pencil is to record distances, such as making a map, or even designing a flower arrangement in the rockery. It is more likely though that it will be for reasons which at first cannot be explained in words, and that we will know by instinct that we need to draw. Each of these reasons will demand a slightly different approach and emphasis. For instance, maps and diagrams usually have the emphasis placed more on line and texture than on tone, whereas a drawing of a misty morning in a wooded valley may be much more concerned with tone and soft edges.

The subject chosen by instinct is the most important one to discuss. In time it will become quickly apparent why we may have been attracted to a particular subject. The type of drawing most useful in this quest is the 'study' which is employed in searching out the reasons why certain subjects affect us. The study is not a technique but an attitude to drawing which has no preconceived image or design. It leaves the artist with complete freedom to discover and try to re-create that which he finds exciting in the chosen subject. Unlike the illustration or map which must conform to specific requirements and is therefore limited, the study is used to sort out problems perhaps relating to a painting or sculpture one may be working on. The objective is not the end product, but the knowledge gained from the artist's scrutiny whilst working. As progress is made some studies will be complete enough and readable enough to exhibit. They are usually much more interesting drawings than those made to a formula and which are very tidy. Perhaps this is due to the exposure of the artist's thinking, which is often concealed in finished illustration. The drawings you make and continue to make (whether you wish to make finished renderings as illustrations or not) should be studies, where each one teaches you something new.

'Finish' in drawing

Many students find themselves in a state of dilemma because of an underlying pressure to produce a finished object. A drawing is finished when it can no longer be developed for the better. It will be correct when you yourself are satisfied that it can progress no further. The distinction between 'finished' and 'correct' lies in the artist's attitude towards drawing rather than any predetermined standards. The finished state is reached when the artist has achieved a drawing which contains something true to the character of the subject which only he can know. The original drawing may be hardly discernable to anyone else, or may be very slight; most probably the finished drawing will be a mixture, with some areas re-worked considerably while others remain unaltered from the first marks.

A finished drawing can often become very tedious and self-conscious the nearer it comes to being a completed object. The work reaches a point where one's desire to recreate becomes confused with imitation. The result is often a mannered technique, which appears to be concerned exclusively with superficial appearances. Perhaps this is because the finished drawing attempts too much, whereas the study takes only one or two aspects of a subject and explores them in depth, giving the work a clarity and unity through its selection.

As well as having the problem of finished drawings to contend with, the novice draughtsman often has the intention of acquiring a 'style'. Once a style or method of drawing has been established, however, it is of limited application. There is no style which one can use for each and every occasion, and any attempt at conforming subject to style will only lead to monotonous reproduction of technique, without thought or virtue. The subject must always suggest the technique and never vice versa. This often happens to those students whose complete reliance on photographic reference for

John Constable. *Pencil study* (British Museum)

21

everything they create produces backward work, which always seems stunted and under-developed. Perhaps this is because the photograph sets up a model which, though it can be reproduced perfectly by the artist, is itself an image of a glance, and contains nothing of real value to the person who wishes to learn the nature of things and their differing aspects and moods. There is no selection and ordering, no re-appraisal of what has been seen, and to my mind photographs remain entirely unrelated to drawing.

The ideas which you hold upon drawing are those which motivate your wish to create. The developing, and questioning, of those ideas will be essential to future progress. As your work advances so too must your ideas. Be careful not to follow blindly behind the conception of others. Retaining your own personality and beliefs in the work you will be producing is fundamental to its progress. For, although you may agree with and respect the conception of others, and may possibly be influenced by them, you are different. You will, if you set about your work seriously, discover that you

Carol Gardner. *Blossom*

The White House. B pencil

can see much better with your own vision. The enduring ingredient of any drawing is that vision that is the artist's very own. Corot, the nineteenth-century French landscape artist, said this:

   . . . be firm, be meek, but follow your own convictions. It is better to be nothing than an echo of other painters.

Considerations

Although choice of subject is entirely up to the individual artist, there are one or two considerations which the newcomer to drawing may find helpful to ponder over. One of these is to remember that as pencil drawing is monochrome, colour cannot be expressed. Should the main attraction of the subject be colour, then a drawing in greys is not going to be very expressive of the main quality which the artist seeks to define.

One's first attempts at working as a draughtsman may be better confined to fairly straightforward inanimate subjects of one or two items which take your fancy around the house, with no colour which is too positive. They should be non-reflective if possible and without too much texture. The time which is available should be kept in mind too. There has been many a potentially good drawing ruined because of a last minute rush to finish; the results are usually quite desperate. The worst thing about this kind of situation is (except under extreme circumstances), it is usually avoidable with a little forethought and planning.

Objects which show their basic geometric forms are ideal for practice. Box shapes, circular shapes such as dishes, jars, anything which has a form you can easily identify with will do. Students used to learn drawing by first copying old master drawings, and once proficient at this they were allowed into the antique room to work from casts of sculptures. Between these stages some made drawings from geometric models. These were the cube, sphere, pyramid, cone and octagon. After the antique room the student would be allowed into the life class. Although this method of learning the craft of drawing is somewhat frowned upon today it had some advantages. A major one being that the student was made aware at a very early stage of the importance of geometry, and of tone in the basic construction and expression of form.

Geometric shapes define the basis of all that we see. Refining and placing these shapes in their right order, and shading them to their relative values, emphasises the illusion of three dimensions. Sometimes an object will be made up of a number of these geometric modules. Identifying these shapes,

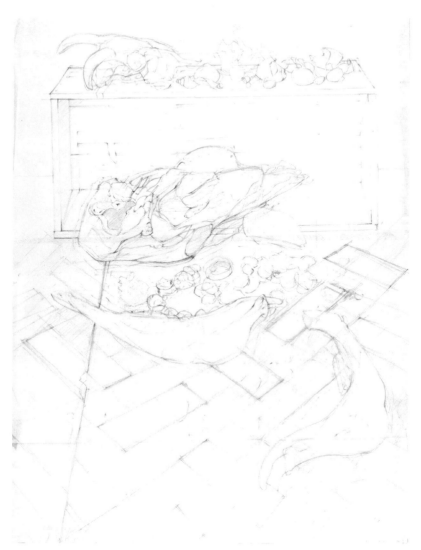

Still life—natural objects   This drawing in line is a study in shape, both positive and negative. The flooring was measured very carefully using the method described and shows the distortion which takes place when an artist tackles a subject which extends beyond the cone of vision.

understanding their proportions, and in the case of more than one object, their relative proportions to each other, is a first consideration.

As I mentioned in the previous chapter the type of work that must be executed to develop visual understanding and the craft of drawing is the study. The slightest sketch should always attempt to reveal something hitherto unknown to the artist; an idle drawing will bring little satisfaction when viewed in retrospect.

To many students 'still life' is utterly repellent. Others are simply not interested, preferring to draw people or landscape. My advice to those students would be – by all means work from these subjects, but at first combine this with a study of still life. The reason is simple: still life is more helpful to the beginner of drawing, and much knowledge can be gained from a static subject bathed in a constant light.

The size of a pencil drawing is a particularly important point for the novice. Because of its nature, pencil is generally used to its best advantage on a fairly small scale. This could be anything up to about Imperial size 570×774 mm ($22\frac{1}{2} \times 30\frac{1}{2}$ in). Anything larger than this tends to become very fussy, especially when there is a lot of detail involved. Also pencil can look very crude on this scale when heavy shading has been used, for it goes very shiny. Of course, there are not set rules for drawing in any medium, but such a large drawing would perhaps be more suitable for a broader medium such as wash or charcoal. A smaller area seems more in keeping with the intimacy pencil can effect.

Organisation in drawing

Once a subject has been decided upon the next consideration is how to present it. If the subject is a straightforward study of one thing without relation to the background, then there is no reason why it should not be placed central to the paper dimensions.

Problems of organisation, or what is called composition, really become evident when more than one object constitutes the subject. Composition is the unifying element in picture making and is both complex and fascinating. It can be a very involved study and though in this short manual few of the basics can be explained, it is an aspect which matures with practice and the study of established paintings. I would recommend further reading on this very important area of drawing.

Composing a drawing or painting means not only arranging the different shapes of the subject in a unified and balanced design, but also organising the distribution of the main light and dark areas. The emphasis on certain linear movements and suggestions in the hope of directing the viewer to look into the picture, not across it, is another basic point to remember.

26

Steelworks. An industrial subject often makes a more interesting study than the 'picturesque'. Notice how the verticals help to balance the horizontal composition and assist in establishing distance. Except for the railway wagons in the foreground such a viewpoint need not involve many perspective problems.

During the process of organising the work in hand it becomes obvious, and necessary, for the artist to be selective in the approach he takes. The art of discrimination as to what exactly is vital to the idea behind what is to be drawn is entirely each individual's decision, and one would find in many cases that each one would claim a different aspect as the one most important to him. As experience is gained the same student would find easier the appreciation of the other's insight and purpose. The reason for this is that there are usually only one or two main aspects of a subject needed to suggest in visual terms its character and function.

Having then briefly identified what composition is, the following points may serve the novice in helping to discover its usefulness and necessity to drawing and painting.

Identifying the main visual structure of a subject is the first stage. Discovering this structure is not too difficult when the subject is drawn in isolation from other objects and whatever background there might be. When the subject constitutes overlapping and partly hidden shapes, transcribing them into flat areas and drawing every shape which can be identified will be of great value in establishing a foundation on which the artist can build up the drawing. This process is often referred to as 'mapping in'.

Looking for the underlying visual essence of a subject the novice must begin by drawing everything. Only by working in this way will he eventually begin to understand the need for, and operate, a selective approach. Studying the work where everything has been attempted is the best way to discover what is unnecessary and what has been overworked or underworked. Once this principle has been grasped the novice can progress to a more rigorously selective approach; for example, by taking only one or two aspects of the subject and concentrating on them. At first it may happen that the artist has chosen the wrong aspect to concentrate on or emphasise. For instance, if the subject is an impressive and solid-looking tree in a local park an outline drawing, however precise, would not express the solidity and mass of the tree. This would be better put over in a tonal drawing; the basic form would emerge as the first factor in establishing the idea the artist wishes to communicate to the viewer, who may not have seen this particular tree.

In order to emphasise the grandeur of such a specimen the artist may decide to contrast this big shape with smaller ones. The most universal measuring unit that we automatically relate things to is the human figure. Placing a figure beside the tree or underneath it immediately sets up a relationship between the two and gives the work scale. Should the artist for any reason not wish to incorporate a figure then animals such as cows or horses may be used. Another possibility worth exploring may be to fill the paper with the form. If a great area of blank paper surrounds the tree, it will immediately reduce the tree's significance and grandeur. Although in such an instance there will be a surrounding terrain of some description, it is important for it to be of less significance than the main subject. This is a problem, especially for the inexperienced. What must be sought is the right balance between the tree and its environment. Playing down secondary interest emphasises the main shapes. However this does not mean that everything else should be hastily sketched in or suggested in an arbitrary fashion. On the contrary the areas of foreground should be carefully related to one another so as to lead the eye into the composition in such a way that is not obvious or crude.

Before putting pencil to paper a few minutes' thought and observation will help the artist decide on his approach, and whether it will be one with a bias towards line, tone, or a fairly even mixture. The most vital characteristics should be considered – shape, movement, line, light and form. The right viewpoint is also worth spending time looking for, as this can enhance a drawing greatly. How much sky? How much foreground, and in the case of still life how much space should surround the objects being studied?

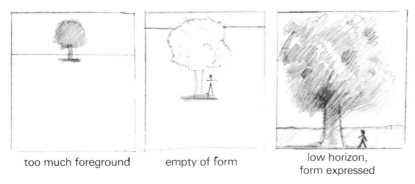

| too much foreground | empty of form | low horizon, form expressed |

Seeking the right balance between the tree and its environment

Composition serves the artist in many ways. The newcomer to drawing however tends to think of it in isolation from reality, believing that it only exists in works of art. This is untrue. Natural compositions can be found quite frequently. It is up to the artist to discover and express them. An old idea sometimes used to help locate possible compositions and separate them from the surrounding areas is the viewfinder, which is simply a rectangle cut from a piece of card leaving a frame which can be looked through. It is similar to looking through a window. The nearer you hold the viewfinder to you the more you can see through it. Holding it at different heights can enable the artist to visualise the effect of having more or less foreground, more or less sky, and where to place the main areas of tone. After a little experience is gained the viewfinder can be discarded, but it can be a help to the beginner.

The novice must not let composition burden him, and though an early awareness of its function is desirable, it is an aspect of drawing which matures slowly. Keeping in mind the intention behind the work will naturally help in the process of developing a composition of unity and clarity.

29

Tone and line

Tone

Tone is used in drawing to express the relative lightness or darkness an object appears to have, as well as helping to describe the form of a subject.

The way which tone or shading is used depends on the artist's intention. It may be used to help express the effects of prevailing light, or it can be used to suggest the three-dimensional nature of objects. Of course, an attempt may be made to express both qualities in the same work.

When the emphasis is to be placed on form there is no need to confuse the issues by trying to explain the tone of the local colour – the local colour being that hue which is predominant, for example the green of an apple. When using tone solely to express form then the colour of the subject may be ignored. The subject is divided into its separate planes, each of which has a tone value. Sometimes these will be the same values or very close. The value of a tone on any single plane varies only as the plane recedes; then the tone becomes lighter. Should the form being studied be cylindrical then the change in tonal value will be expressed gradually.

Establishing the right tones to be used in a painting can be facilitated greatly by studies made in monochrome. The atmosphere tone can suggest is perhaps its greatest asset. Not only can it be used to express form in a mechanical way, but also, with practice and care, it can be used in describing the tones of colour and cast shadows which help in establishing the fall of light on a subject. The effect light has on everything sets a mood, always vital in painting. The biggest problem for anyone new to drawing and painting is that they feel the need to draw 'light' when it is impossible – all that can be drawn is the effect it has on whatever it falls upon, or does not. It is a similar problem to that of drawing water. Again only the effect it has can be shown, that is, how much it distorts what it is flowing across, and its own distortion from a flat plane.

The wholeness that tone can provide assists the artist in setting an atmosphere to the work in progress and without it there can be no suggestion of light. However, to many students of drawing, tone seems to

Study of a cow's skull seen from the underside. It is drawn with 2B and 3B pencils

mean heavy black areas of solid pencil. A process of tonal selection must be practised if the drawing is to have unity. By establishing the big changes in tonal value at the outset it will be easier to consider the amount of detail these larger shapes need to form a convincing and readable representation.

A row of books on a shelf will probably vary considerably in colour. All of the edges will be on the same plane. If an even light is falling on them how are they separated? One may draw them simply by noting the changes between the separate books and the form of the vertical plane where some books are further away from the eye, others nearer. This would suffice to express the form. Should the tone of colour also be drawn however, this would add more character to the individual editions and also set up a potentially more interesting tonal pattern, or structure, to the work.

The point to remember here is that the tonal difference between the individual books results from the tones of local colour, and not change in light conditions. Restraint should be exercised when applying the shading, and it is worth remembering that the darkest colours are never quite as black as at first glance – and the lightest never as light.

Cast shadows created by objects, but not a part of them, can play important roles in studies and compositions. They can help to establish such things as time of day, especially in landscape work; but the major function of the cast shadow is to anchor forms to the horizontal plane. This is most apparent when a figure is sitting on the type of spindly chair often used at table; without the shadows, these chairs and their unfortunate occupants appear to be in the process of being whisked away by a poltergeist!

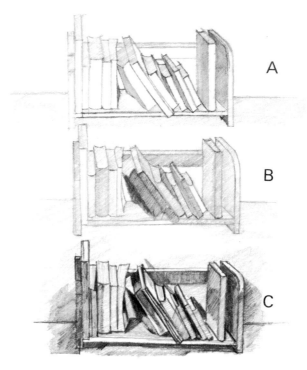

Tone

a. This shows how 'shading' or tone can be used in its simplest form. Each flat plane has a different tone value, separating it from the others not on its own plane. Light effects are not considered; there are no shadows.

b. Shading is used here to describe changes in the tone of local colour. The darkest tone represents the lowest tone of the darkest book, the lightest a white book. Again no attempt at light effects has been made.

c. This is total use of tone; both form and the tone of local colour are suggested. It shows, too, the importance of cast shadows, not only as an aid to suggesting the flat planes of the book stand and table top, but their significance in helping to create chiaroscuro and atmosphere. When you wish to express light—look for the darks.

There are occasions when the omission of cast shadows is desirable, as at times they can destroy form. When this is the case it is usually self-evident and the student must refrain from being too literal, putting it in because 'it is there'.

As in music, tonal scales are often used to set a prevailing atmosphere or mood to a painting. Making drawings to work out these scales can be very useful. A low key drawing may use only part of the full range of tone values from black to middle greys, and a light key drawing will use those at the opposite end of the scale where the darkest 'note' would be represented by a middle grey – the lightest by the paper tone. Of course, there are numerous variations; one may use only black and the paper tone to achieve a dramatic effect. When a drawing uses the full range of tone values the artist must not allow the drawing to lose its unity. Too many tonal values can fragment a drawing and also give it a greyness which can result in flatness. Practising different combinations of the range will help an understanding of tone. It is a good idea to limit the range to three or four to begin with.

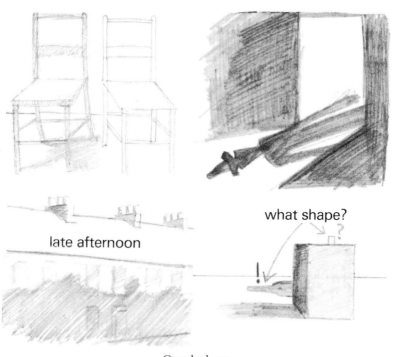

what shape?

late afternoon

Cast shadows

33

Study of a bush. Carbon pencil. The texture apparent in this drawing relies on an attempt to particularize the detail of form, and not on pencil 'technique'.

Line

Although there are no lines which actually encase objects, it is a device which has been used for thousands of years to communicate the concept of shape on flat surfaces. It is a convention common to all periods of art history, perhaps because it is a particularly good way of communicating where changes of shape occur. The line is as precise a medium as we have discovered for describing the world we live in, and for planning its future.

Lines and their combinations are responsible for much of the dynamism at the heart of drawing. Not only the visible and obvious dynamism, but the more subtle movements of an underlying less evident geometric structure, which can be traced in all the greatest paintings. Returning however to the visible attributes of line, there are many characteristics a line may take, and it would be as well to mention some of those here. The effect a straight line has when drawn parallel to one of the edges of a piece of paper is totally different from the effect when drawn diagonally from corner to corner. Depending on the proportions which you have divided the paper into, a relationship is immediately set up between the two parts. This can be a balanced

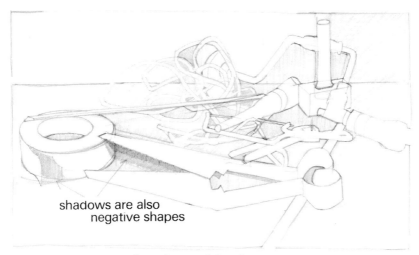

shadows are also
negative shapes

Secondary modules of a picture

proportion or an imbalanced one. Perpendicular and horizontal divisions are usually best made between unequal areas of space. However the proportions one to the other should never be too extreme unless for a specific purpose. Dividing a rectangle by a diagonal into two equal areas is much more successful and pleasing, because it creates two new shapes – triangles which are related to the rectangle of the paper. Though a rectangle divided with perpendicular and horizontal lines creates new shapes their relationship to the whole is not so contrasted or dynamic as the creation of two brand new shapes, as with a diagonal.

Lines can have character, for example a wavering line may help suggest a feeling of uncertainty or insecurity. A broken zig-zag line can suggest nervous energy; the lilting, even curvature of a line can be used in the portrayal of graceful actions. All of these characteristics may be suggested by the subject which is under scrutiny, but it is as well to be aware of their potential, in order to discover them.

Many textures are made up from a series of lines placed in such relationships as to form patterns. Cross-hatching, short vertical or horizontal strokes and short uneven and broken lines can all be structured to create texture. The student of drawing would be wise to practise these methods of creating texture on scraps of paper, and look around to discover the type of subject this texture would relate to.

The modelled line is particularly useful but nevertheless limited in some respects. It is used frequently in figure drawing and is used primarily to assist in the suggestion of form, and distance. The principle that governs its use is that the nearer a form is to the spectator the stronger the line is which is used to express that form. On occasions an edge may be almost indiscernable and at these times would be made slight or perhaps broken, even non-existent. The times when these differing qualities of line are suitable will be suggested by studying the subject carefully, and experimenting in a positive way. Look for edges which contrast with the background; light objects against a dark background will be very distinct, yet if the foreground object partly overlaps another light area the weight of line used at that point will be less distinct.

For short exercises collect together a number of articles which have something in common with each other. Garden tools, kitchen untensils, pans and pots or anything which is not obviously something beautiful. Pick them from the point of view of a draughtsman and vary the shapes as much as possible. Set them up on a board which can be moved easily without disturbing their arrangement. Whilst arranging them stay aware of the cast shadows and negative shapes. Arrange the group with a fairly strong light directed from the side. Position yourself just over a metre (about four feet) from the subject and if you have no easel prop the board on your knees and rest it on the back of another chair. When you begin to draw pay most attention to the cast shadows and negative shapes. Do not bother about any 'shading' which may be on the objects. Pay particular attention to the character of the shadows; whether they have hard distinct edges or soft and diffused ones, and how black they are, or whether they vary in tone, not only from each other but in themselves. This exercise is useful in that it will help you to understand that the subject creates other shapes, and that when drawing or painting one cannot ignore the secondary modules of a picture.

Chiaroscuro is the treatment of light and shade, and is very important to those who wish to continue their studies into painting. One of the great exponents of chiaroscuro was Rembrandt. In many of his works whole groups of figures are painted in dark close tonal values, and set against contrasting areas of light close tonal values. The individuality of the shapes which form the masses are identified by colour and temperature rather than by delineation or tone. The mass of dark areas is often relieved by the introduction of light passages at significant points. Copying this type of painting with pencil and analysing the importance of tonal structure will help the student to discover these qualities for himself in nature.

Outside

When it comes to drawing out of doors or away from the convenience of the home, one can feel very isolated at first; whether in a remote spot or in the centre of a busy city. Reconciling yourself to the fact that you are really working and not simply enjoying a leisurely activity amidst all the business of the commercial world is difficult, especially when you become surrounded by curious onlookers. However, confining your creative activities to the home or evening class environment can narrow your outlook to some extent. So a thick skin must be acquired, and a belief that what you are doing, whether it be full-time or part-time, is valid to everyone else just as much as it is to yourself. In time the mundane and continually predictable questions and questioners will become less of a deterrent.

There are many good subjects which are available; and often not a great distance from base. Getting out and about with a sketch book is a rewarding activity. Apart from being healthy in a physical sense, drawing out of doors keeps your mind alive to the changing light effects. This continual process can often reveal different aspects of a subject.

Many students find this constant change a drawback rather than a help, and of course it does have its negative side. However, I believe the advantages easily outweigh the disadvantages in that one must be alert and aware of these changes occurring. It is easier to draw indoors. The constant light on a subject, and the attendant comforts of indoor study, can lead to an over-relaxed attitude with the consequence that the work may become complacent as well. This is true more in the case of novices than the more experienced. The endless change apparent when out of doors has the effect of keeping the senses sharpened and responsive to those occurrences which can be used for the benefit of a drawing.

Another advantage of the changing conditions is that they give a drawing a feeling of immediacy and intimacy with the atmosphere of time and place. Such a drawing, no matter how slight, almost inevitably retains something real and truthful, whereas work which is carried on isolated from the outside can be much more prone to academic dogma and technicalities.

Townscape

When work in town is planned, drawing buildings or street scenes, a viewpoint which takes in too little is almost as bad as one which takes in too much. Enough of the surrounding environment should be chosen in order that a true representation may be given. Keep in mind that a clue to scale must be given, and so objects like pillar boxes and doorways, though not vital, are better put in than not, especially when no figures are going to be used.

Roadways, which will be a major part of a townscape, must help in leading the viewer into the composition and not across it. Avoid views through archways and passages until experience is gained. The archway especially is a subject which is more in keeping with the postcard of local architecture than drawing; it can make a drawing too evenly structured, making the finished work appear as a stage set.

One of the most useful ways of beginning a drawing of buildings is with a horizontal or vertical edge. This has the advantage that angles of perspective can be much easier to establish. A 90-degree angle is fairly straightforward and any mistake is easily identified and corrected. Both the horizontals and verticals can be established by relating them to the edges of the paper. Of course it is vital that the paper has regular 90-degree corners, and is square on the drawing board. Once this cross is established all the other angles can be measured against it with the measuring stick. Verticals, unless an extreme viewpoint is taken (looking up a building's walls or down them), generally

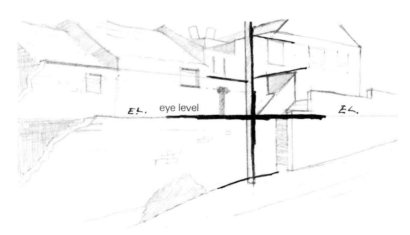

It is important to begin a perspective drawing by establishing two constants; a vertical and a horizontal to form a cross. All of the angles representing the roof, steps and slope of the road can be found by relating them to these two constants.

remain as verticals as far as perspective is concerned. However, the only definite horizontal is at eye level, and unfortunately this will not always correspond to an actual horizontal line through the subject.

Establishing the biggest shapes should be the next stage. Once these are working and the basic forms of the structures are related, it is only a matter of careful deliberation to complete the drawing in as much detail as is required. The same process is used at this stage as at the first, taking the verticals or horizontals of the details and working out relative angles from them.

The student should beware of drawing things which are known to be a part of the actual fabric of buildings when in fact they are not visually apparent. It is important to draw from observation, and not knowledge of how buildings are constructed. Looking for the quintessential visual information about the building's character and its environment under the prevailing light conditions will help enormously in portraying the atmosphere of place. The newcomer to drawing and painting has one problem greater than any other: thinking in 'actualities' rather than 'visualities'. For instance, a bright light falling on a wall will to a certain extent break up the regular pattern of brickwork, so it will only exist in visual terms at certain points on the wall. Shadows reflected in windows will change as the sun moves around. Look for what is, not how you think it should be, and ask yourself 'is it visible, or do I just know it exists?'

Perspective

Perspective is an area much ignored by present students, especially those who unfortunately have little time for study. However, a familiarity with its principal points will facilitate a better understanding and swifter recognition of observed shape, especially in the drawing of buildings. Knowing its principles is also a great advantage in the composing of pictures. It is an exact science though, and many artists feel it is superfluous to their aesthetic beliefs. There are great works of art which completely ignore the principles of perspective, but because it is an exact science its rules must be obeyed if the artist wishes to achieve a convincing representation of proportion and depth.

Perspective assumes we see with one eye and that it is stationary; however, our one eye has the joint cone of vision of both. It also assumes that all lines (or planes) parallel to the ground plane, when seen from a fixed view, appear to converge on a point or points on the horizon. These points are known as the vanishing points. It also assumes that perpendicular planes (or lines) appear to diminish in size the farther away they are from the observer, i.e. the nearer to the horizon they are. Those planes (or lines) which are not parallel to the ground plane have their vanishing points on the horizon of their own planes.

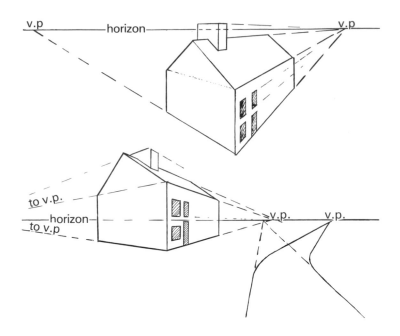

The cone of vision is the maximum field of view which can be seen without moving the head. It spans 60 degrees, that is 30 degrees each way from the centre line of vision. When an object is focused upon, the centre of vision runs directly from the eyes to the object.

The picture plane is an imaginary vertical plane which the cone of vision passes through, when a subject is viewed, and lies between the observer and the subject. It stands exactly parallel to the observer's face and never at an angle. All points pass through this plane on the way to the eye of the observer. It is this plane that the picture is painted from, i.e. all points passing through the picture plane should correspond proportionately with the exact same points of reference on the artist's canvas. The picture plane is extremely important to an understanding of the principals of perspective.

The ground plane is the horizontal plane which the observer's feet are standing on. The horizon of the ground plane corresponds with the eye level of the observer. The ground line is the edge of the horizontal ground plane.

Eye level is the level at which the observer views the subject. There is only one eye level in a conventional, representational drawing of a given subject. Eye level coincides with the horizon of the ground plane, which always runs parallel to it, irrespective of the terrain within the cone of vision of the artist, i.e. between observer and subject.

A person on a beach looking out to sea has coinciding with his eye level the horizon of the sea. Another person standing nine metres (30 ft) above on the edge of a cliff looking out to sea also has an eye level corresponding with the horizon of the sea. However, the person who is higher can see a great deal more sea than the person on the beach below. The reason that the sea's horizon will always coincide with that of the observer's eye level is that the sea always remains parallel to the ground plane of the observer. As has already been mentioned all planes parallel to that of the ground plane of the observer will have their horizon line on that of the observer's eye level.

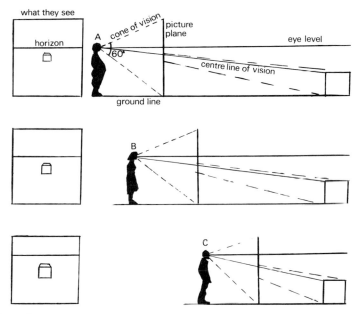

Picture plane

The nearer the picture plane is to the subject the larger the subject will be projected. The three observers all focus on to the nearest top horizontal edge of the same cube. Man 'A' has a more panoramic view than woman 'B' who in turn sees more of her surroundings than man 'C'.

Anything lying outside the cone of vision where it cuts the picture plane will be distorted if a perspective is attempted. The nearer the station point is to the picture plane the narrower the angle of vision becomes. The picture plane can be against the subject, but it is important that the observer is not too near the picture plane. The angle of 60 degrees marks the boundary of focus, so make sure all you wish to include in a drawing lies within that angle. If it does not you may have to step further back from the subject.

Only the objects which fall within the angle of 60 degrees from the station point can be suitably represented in perspective drawings, without distortion.

41

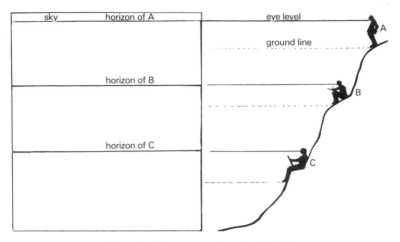

The relationship between eye level and the horizon

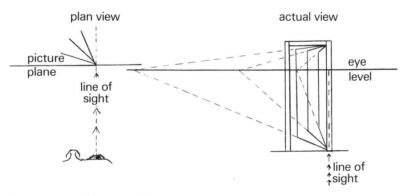

An open door in perspective
The observer stands immediately in line with the right-hand door jamb. While the door remains closed it is seen parallel to the picture plane of the observer. As the door is opened it moves away from the parallel plane and into an angular plane in relation to the picture plane. As the plane of the door swings towards the centre line of vision it can be observed that the vanishing point in turn must move towards the centre line of vision. The greater the angle of a line to the picture plane, the steeper the receding lines to the horizon will be. If the door were to open towards the observer it would cut through the ground line of the picture plane. When this happens the vanishing point would be shifted to the right of the centre of vision and would remain at eye level. Vanishing points always remain behind the picture plane, and are never located behind the observer.

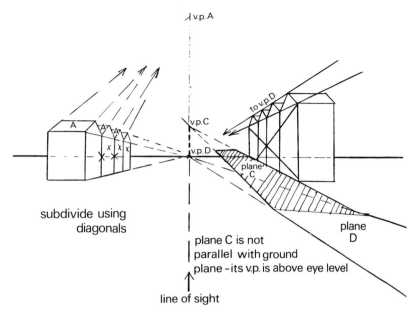

v.p.A

v.p.C

to v.p.D

v.p.D

plane C

subdivide using
diagonals

plane D

plane C is not
parallel with ground
plane - its v.p. is above eye level

line of sight

Inclined planes

Planes not horizontal and inclined away from the artist have their vanishing points located above that of the horizon line of the artist. Declining planes correspondingly will have their vanishing points located below the horizon of the artist's eye level.

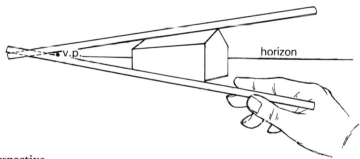

v.p.

horizon

Perspective

To locate the vanishing point of a subject first establish where the horizon line intersects the buildings or forms. Imagine the forms are made of perspex and that you can see through them. The horizon line will always be at eye level. Take the nearest corner of a building then hold out the measuring stick so that it corresponds to the line of the eyes. Make a note as to where you think the measuring stick coincides with the horizon line on your paper. Then move it round so it corresponds with the line where the wall meets the ground. Where the two points meet on the horizon line is the location of the vanishing point. As the drawing progresses you may find slight adjustments necessary.

The only way of making very precise perspective drawings is by use of T-squares, scaled measurements, plans and elevations. Though easy to carry out it is a very lengthy process which involves projection and much technical perspiration. An architect's text book is a good purchase for those students wishing to construct perspectives from unusual viewpoints. If the rules explained in these few pages are adhered to, and the method of measuring angles and distance is followed, the student should find no great difficulty in rendering perspectives of all but the most complicated of shapes.

A view in parallel perspective

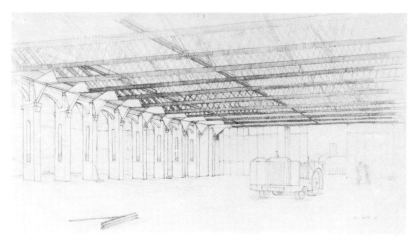

Perspective study. HB pencil. The vertical columns narrow the further away they are from the observer.

Malvern Hills. B pencil

The introduction of figures helps to establish scale in a drawing

The figure

Heads, hands and feet

Possibly the most demanding, as well as rewarding, subject of study is the human figure. Throughout the history of art the representation of the human form has been a constant inspiration to artists. Of all images, it is the supreme vehicle for expressing our deepest emotions. The possibilities and incentives offered by its study are immense, and make it the most sublime subject available to the artist.

For many students anatomy is something which they consider they ought to be knowledgeable about before any attempt is made at figure drawing. Anatomy, like perspective, can be an obvious assistance to drawing. However, in both cases they are not essential. Observation is much more important, and through observation a knowledge of the role of anatomy will be acquired. Studying living models, rather than diagrams of perfect 'specimens' of the human form will benefit the fine-artist much more.

It is the artist's response to real and living subjects which is important. In many cases muscles are concealed or under-developed; the majority of the populace are not endowed with physiques in which the muscles are as well-defined as in anatomy books. What is important in figure drawing from observation is the describing of actual and visible form, and not the correcting of that form into a predetermined visual structure which conforms to a scheme determining what is and what is not visible. If the artist is concerned with the visual world, his response to, and reappraisal of it, then it is in the visual terms which he must express that reappraisal. This is not to say that anatomy is unimportant to a study of figure drawing, but that its usefulness is limited.

As I mentioned earlier, laying down flat shapes, in the correct sequence and proportions to each other, and rightly toned, creates an illusion of three dimensions (or form). Figure drawing demands the finest degree of accuracy in these relationships. The terms which are used for its description must be consistent if the work is going to hold together. There is no place for incongruous and superficial marks. The most wispy of drawings made by a

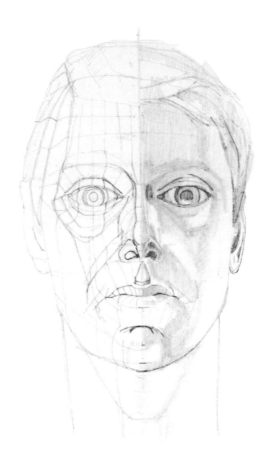

The head
The planes of the head explain its form. On the left contour lines show how they fit together. The right-hand side shows how tone and its emphasis at corresponding changes of form can help to suggest these changes in a more sophisticated 'diagram', or 'map'.

master contain many years of accumulated knowledge, both of the subject and the craft. These drawings can look deceptively simple in their conciseness, but it would not be wise to base first studies on such work, as it will only lead to a second-hand slickness of execution.

Although the subject will contain elements of contour, form and chiaroscuro, perhaps initially it would be profitable to concentrate on one of these aspects. I would suggest trying to explain the form. Although artists have been successful in suggesting form by line only, this approach is limited and success will only be achieved with the passing of time and the knowledge only experience can teach us. A tonal approach using line in a clarifying role to pick out those areas where tone is insufficient, and to emphasise an edge or contour, would be the most sensible approach for the novice.

When drawing form the need is to signify where changes in that form take place, and the nature of the change. A head contains many changes in plane; sometimes these will be obvious. The change from the cheek to the side of the nose is a major change of plane. The largest change of plane which occurs on the head is from the side to the front of the cheek. This is the first change of plane that should be established and is the main factor in creating the basic form or roundness of the head.

It is, though, the more subtle changes of plane which continue to confuse artists. The curve of the mouth or the gentle undulations of eyelids can be most elusive to identify. Both lips and eyes are more positive colours than the skin colour and it is often this which confuses the inexperienced. Again it is the problem of transcribing colour into tone. The student would be best advised when figure drawing to look carefully at these particular points and remember the principle of drawing in monochrome is to express form, and not colour.

Placing the sitter in a good light will be half the battle won when the study of form is intended. This light can be established by placing the sitter by a window without any other artificial light falling on the subject from other directions. Daylight is much softer than artificial light and there are no substitutes for it, no matter what the manufacturers tell us about 'real daylight' bulbs and tubes.

There are many viewpoints from which a head can be drawn. To begin to get to know its structure in more positive visual terms I would suggest taking straight on views of full face and profile. Possibly the most difficult view is the three-quarter view; until the novice is conversant with the structure of the head it would be wise to lay this viewpoint aside for the beginning. As the craft of drawing is gained, the need to experiment and investigate more complex problems of viewpoint and lighting will become apparent.

Once the pose and viewpoint are decided and the model is comfortable the drawing is begun. Lightly indicating the main areas of shade and plane changes can be one of the most advantageous beginnings. The basic form begins to emerge and nothing is too boldly stated. The reason for this tentative beginning is to place the head in as pleasing a relationship as possible to the edges of the paper. Should an outline form the beginnings of such a study, it would have the disadvantage of being too definite a statement. It can become a barrier to the novice, because it is a statement which many find difficult to alter once it has been made. It also has the disadvantage that the

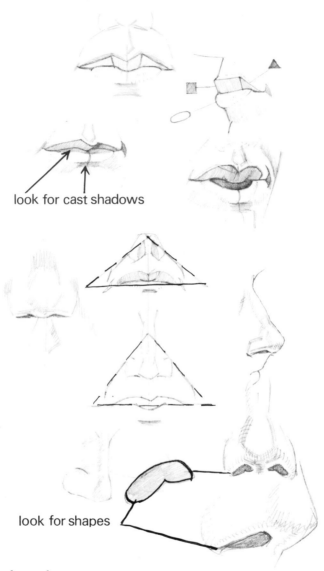

look for cast shadows

look for shapes

Nose and mouth

An area as subtle as the nose and mouth cannot be explored in any depth without being drawn fairly large. A drawing of a head 5 cm (2 in) in width cannot hope to 'explain' as much about its details as one three times the size. The scale of a drawing must be taken into account if the artist is intent on more than suggestion. To draw anything it must first be understood, if you do not understand the structure of a nose or mouth inspect the area at closer range.

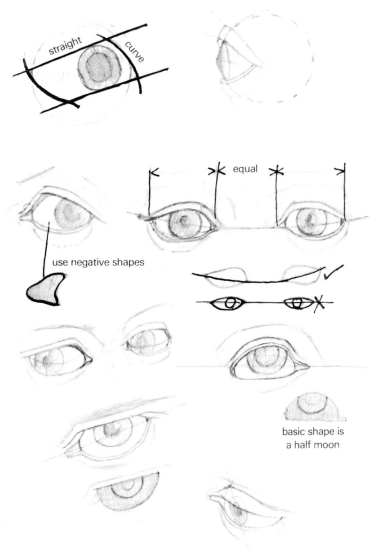

use negative shapes

equal

basic shape is
a half moon

Eyes

At the outer corner of the eye it can be observed that the lids meet at a point further around the circumference of the eyeball than where they meet beside the nose. This is most apparent when drawn from above. The most common schema for positioning eyes is that which begins by establishing them the distance of an eye apart when drawn straight on; adjustments can be easily made once a foundation head is established. The thickness of eyelids should always be noted. The top lids always overlap the bottom at the corners. The eyeball will always remain a sphere; only the iris becomes an ellipse when viewed at an angle. When the lids are 'normal'; that is when the eyes are not animated, they overlap the iris slightly.

51

features are often 'adapted' in order to fit into the outline. Allow the form of the head to emerge by directing the growth of tonal values. They express the form, help to unify the features, and keep the drawing from fragmenting into disjointed relationships between silhouette and form.

When the main areas of tone are stated, the relative positions of the features are indicated. The measuring stick is particularly useful in establishing these points. The horizontal and vertical distances between points such as the corners of the eyes compared to the length of the bridge of the nose should be stated accurately. Distances from ear to ear, width of mouth and so on should all be checked using the measuring stick when in doubt. The measuring stick can also be helpful in checking whether a point is lying 'under' or beside a corresponding point and is used to 'plumb' the drawing into its correct shape and form. Too often the student finds that he is drawing a detail in absolute isolation from the other details which causes them to become separated and unrelated to one another. Standing back from the drawing and comparing it to the subject is a practice many students fail to avail themselves of. Its advantage lies in the fact that the drawing is looked at in its entirety and compared to the whole subject. A great many students, (and more experienced artists) suffer from not doing this. The remark 'this bit really works well, compared with the rest' is one frequently made during the discussion of drawings.

When the basic tonal pattern and proportions are fixed, it is time to begin searching out and describing the idiosyncracies of the sitter. It is at this point that the majority of students' work literally begins to go to pieces. Swopping from detail to detail without regard to the whole, the student embarks on the destruction of the form that is emerging. Part of the reason for this disuniting process is the obsession many beginners have for 'getting likenesses'. A superficial likeness can be achieved with the camera much better and without trauma. It is much more in keeping with artistic heritage and licence for the draughtsman to investigate that likeness, and attempt to discover how it can be used by way of emphasis or subtlety to say something about personality. It should be an aspect of drawing that emerges as the drawing grows, or does not; and not the only consideration. Take a good look at any cartoon of a public personality – you may be suprised to find that it does not 'look' like him at all!

To a greater or lesser extent we all draw from memory, we cannot look both at our drawing and subject whilst working. A great many students glance up and down from subject to drawing. Although this may be all right for a few students, for most it is a tiring activity which is quite unnecessary. Looking a little bit longer and understanding the shape to be drawn will enable the student to attempt its whole shape and not only a section of it.

Taking in the complex shapes involved in figure drawing needs more time than a glance; the mental picture from a longer look is retained not only more vividly but for a considerably longer time. Comprehending the true shapes is paramount to recreating them. Once this is understood actual drawing time is increased and less time is spent glancing from subject to paper.

Looking for clues which help to identify and explain form is an important aspect of figure drawing. The more obvious of these are watch straps, folds which fall around the form, necklaces, waist bands and trouser bottoms. They are useful in that they suggest the cross-section of the form they are concealing. In the drawing of nude figures, a bracelet or other jewellery is sometimes worn by the model; this can be capitalised on in the same way. Other cross-sections can be suggested by creases in the actual flesh, such as around the waist when the model is sitting; should an arm be bent the join of forearm to upper arm can be seen as a part cross-section. One should ask oneself the question: 'What is it that tells me in visual terms, from this viewpoint, about the shape of that form?'

Many students have problems with the drawing of hands. They can look very strange when foreshortened or seen from unusual angles. One of the best ways to learn about them is to pose the hands in action, either holding something or gesticulating. A hand posed flat on its palm is in just about the most difficult position to be drawn, and this should be avoided until a knowledge of its structure is gained. Another point about hands is their size. When opened and compared to the face, they will generally span the distance from chin to top of brow. Women have smaller, more delicate hands than men, and artists sometimes emphasise this delicacy by drawing them smaller than they may in fact be. Making men's hands too small is a common oversight and if there is to be a bias towards one or the other, then for the drawing of the male, the hands work better if they are drawn larger.

The same size relationships occur with feet. Drawing feet as carefully as possible and checking angles and distances is the only way to learn about them. Too many students skate around the problem of feet and consider their importance worth only a brief outline. As with hands, posing the feet in action can be of great assistance. Getting to know about hands and feet will be greatly facilitated by making studies of them life size, and not as big as a big toe nail as many students do!

major changes established

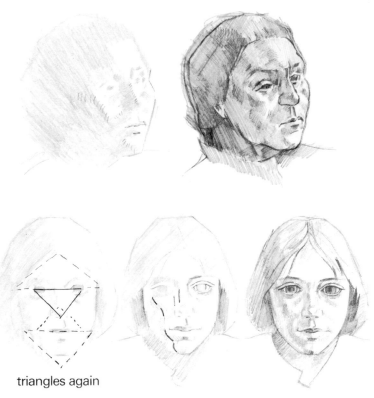

triangles again

Heads

These are the three most common views that the portrait painter uses. Learn how to establish the form of the head by taking direct full, three-quarter or profile views. Viewpoints between these three are difficult, even for experienced draughtsmen.

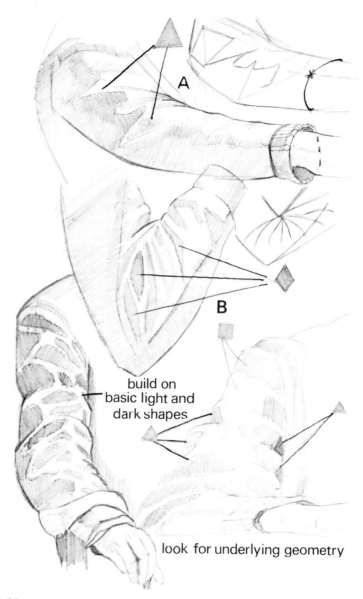

build on
basic light and
dark shapes

look for underlying geometry

Folds

In these studies of folds notice how the ellipse of the garment helps to suggest the cross-section of the form. The tone often becomes slightly darker when a change of plane is imminent—as can be seen in the top drawing. Folds often form a concertina pattern, pulled outwards (a) or pushed inwards (b).

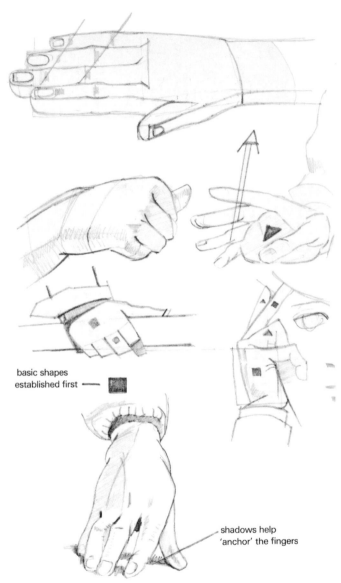

basic shapes
established first ——

shadows help
'anchor' the fingers

Hands

The most important aspect of hands is their basic form. A good way to discover this form is to draw hands with fairly tight-fitting gloves on them. This serves to conceal those details which often distract the beginner and cause confusion. Similarly, drawing stockinged feet is a useful exercise until the essentials are understood. Look for overlapping lines (a).

56

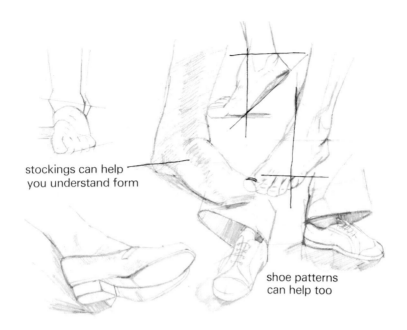

stockings can help
you understand form

shoe patterns
can help too

The full figure

The first consideration should be how large to draw the figure. If a fairly detailed study is intended the figure should be made as large as possible. It will also be necessary to be quite close to the model, keeping in mind that going too close will create the problem of not being able to conceive the whole figure within the cone of vision (that is, without moving the head). A distance of about three metres (10 ft), or twice the distance you stand in front of a mirror to view your new clothes in, would be the right distance. Should the intention be to relate the figure to its immediate surroundings the distance should be increased to a point where the entire subject can be viewed as a whole, without moving the head. Relating the model to the background in drawings is of special significance to painters as this is the recurring problem in any objective painting.

All artists evolve a particular way of progressing with a drawing. However, at the beginning one must trust to others' suggestions as to how to begin. It does not really matter at which point on the body a study of a full figure begins. There is no reason why the process of drawing the head in the previous pages should not be followed for the full figure and the big changes related first. Sometimes this may not be practicable, especially if the model has been placed in a poor light. In these cases a drawing may be better begun by suggesting as accurately as possible the main directions of the limbs and torso until the figure's form begins to make itself more easily understood, which will happen as a natural result of looking at it for any length of time. Daumier, the nineteenth-century French artist, used a technique which at first glance looks very loose and free. The form is created by a great many flowing lines which help create a feeling of rhythm and movement.

Tintoretto, another great master of expressing action through the rhythm of his drawings, is certainly worth study, and a comparison of the two will be sufficient for the student to see that each artist expresses a similar feeling in quite different ways. Space does not permit a reproduction of samples of these artists' work, but a local library would most certainly contain an edition with plates of examples. A number of artists prefer to begin at a central point on the figure, perhaps the navel or an area of particular interest to the draughtsman, and work out from this, carefully plotting a course across the form by selecting key changes of plane or line. The drawing is steadily built up working from one small area to the next. The disadvantage of this particular way of describing form is that tone is a secondary consideration and rarely used. It is a very precise and demanding technique to study by, and not until one has spent some time on the drawing does it begin to come together as a relationship of shapes, expressive of form. The same type of progression can be achieved by using both line and tone and has the advantage that the form 'appears' much sooner, as will the mistakes which need rectifying.

The usefulness of geometric schemata in drawing figures and heads has been explored by many artists. The most popular is that which bases the human form on a cylindrical system. This is where each limb, the torso and head are first expressed in a very crude geometry. A method used by Durer was based on square modules. Although these schemata are interesting in the quest for the ideal proportion and drawing from one's imagination, I have found them limited when used in the life-room. Deciphering the tones of a figure into flat geometric shapes, however, can be a great help in setting out proportion and establishing contour. This type of study is often begun at a central point of interest.

These are but a few of the many ways a drawing may begin. My reason for mentioning a number rather than my own preference is to show that there is no 'right way' to draw – there is only a right approach. Methods vary from artist to artist. The common denominator of all of these approaches however is that they are all methods by which the figure is studied and investigated. They are analytical approaches to drawing which by their application and practice enable the artist to make an 'attractive' drawing at will, should he wish. The strange thing is that artists rarely make 'attractive' drawings. What they do make are drawings which have taught them something of significance about the visual world which inspires speculation by many others should they have the fortune to see them.

As long as the student retains that necessary integrity of purpose and enthusiasm, then the rewards of discovery and appreciation of many visions will be enjoyed. The student will also, with luck, contribute to the tradition and excellence of true draughtsmanship.

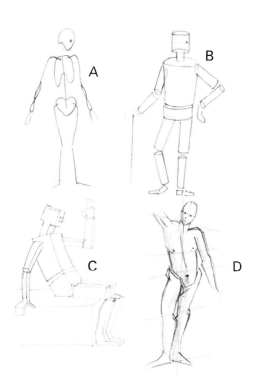

Schemata

These are the four most common modules which form the basis on which proportions and pose are established. 'D' is perhaps the most immediate. The centre line is established first, then large changes in direction and tone. Note that the centre line runs from the neck to the ankle where the most weight is carried. This is common to all free-standing poses where the weight is unevenly distributed between the two feet.

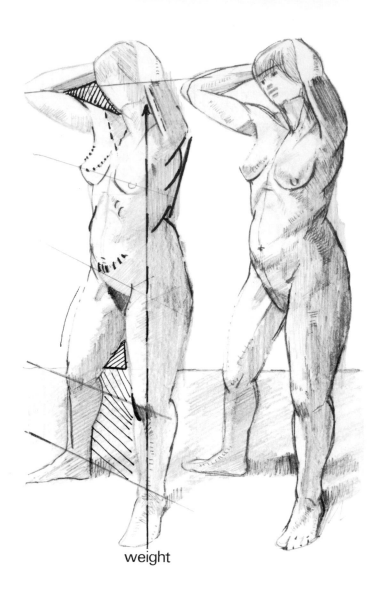

weight

This study was begun by first establishing the pose. It was most important to find where the main weight was distributed, i.e. under the neck. Notice too, that figure drawing must adhere to the laws of perspective. As with drawing heads, the main changes of plane are expressed by a change in tonal values at the outset. Care has been taken in looking for overlapping lines and disappearing lines. Negative shapes once again come in useful for establishing the correct angles of arms and legs.

Standing nude. B pencil

Costume study. HB pencil

Portrait. HB pencil

Tonal study. 2B and 3B pencil. The big changes in light and dark help to establish the foreshortening of the form.

Corot. *Reclining figure of a young girl* (British Museum)